THE PROPERTY VO

PROPERTY INVESTOR TOOLKIT

A 7-Part Toolkit for Property Investment Success

Brought to You By

Richard W J Brown

THE PROPERTY VOICE

www.thepropertyvoice.net

The Property Voice - Property Investor Toolkit

DISCLAIMER

This disclaimer governs the use of this ebook. By using this ebook, you accept this disclaimer in full.

This book is designed to provide helpful information and inspiration to readers about property investing. The information is not advice, and should not be treated as such. The content is the sole expression and opinion of the author. It is provided with the understanding that neither the author nor publisher is engaged to render any type of professional advice. References are provided for informational purposes only and do not constitute endorsement of any websites or other sources. Readers should be aware that the websites listed in this book may change. Readers are advised to use the material contained within this book in a safe and logical manner. You must not rely on the information in the ebook as an alternative to legal, financial, investment, taxation, accountancy, or other advice from an appropriately qualified professional. If you have any specific questions about any aforementioned matter, you should consult an appropriately qualified professional.

To the maximum extent permitted by applicable law below, we exclude all representations, warranties, undertakings and guarantees relating to the ebook. We will not be liable to you in respect of any losses arising out of any event or events beyond our reasonable control.

We will not be liable to you in respect of any business losses, including without limitation loss of or damage to profits, income, revenue, use, production, anticipated savings, business, contracts, commercial opportunities or goodwill.

We will not be liable to you in respect of any loss or corruption of any data, database or software.

We will not be liable to you in respect of any special, indirect or consequential loss or damage.

This disclaimer will be governed by and construed in accordance with English law, and any disputes relating to this disclaimer will be subject to the exclusive jurisdiction of the courts of England and Wales.

Contents

Introduction

The Toolkit is as an aid to investors, new or experienced, for the use in considering their ideal property investment journey, assessing potential property investments individually or as a portfolio and a bunch of other resources along the way. In this first version, you will find the following sections looking at the 'property investment lifecycle' of starting out as a property investor:

1. Property investing strategy selection
2. Property investing criteria & calculations
3. Property investing research tools
4. Property-related reading lists & communities
5. Lettings & property management
6. Property financials
7. Property as an investment
8. Summary & next steps
9. eBook only bonuses

The Toolkit is not a comprehensive 'how-to' guide; it is a starting place for new investors to refer to and a reminder for more experienced investors to crosscheck against. Please do subscribe to our mailing list at www.thepropertyvoice.net to get news of the Toolkit updates, monthly newsletters and one or two other subscriber-only goodies along the way. If you bought the paperback version of the Toolkit you will notice that external links are not written in full. If you would like a copy of the PDF file format along with a list of all the fully functioning and clickable external links, then please follow the process outlined in Section 9. You will receive not only the PDF version of the book but also a number of extra bonuses. To claim your PDF version and extra bonuses, note this code: **Toolkit Bonus 15/01**

I hope you enjoy the Property Investor Toolkit.

Richard W J Brown
The Property Voice

Section 1
Property Investing Strategy Selection

As this is a Toolkit, the idea is to get you thinking rather than provide an in-depth explanation and analysis. That said there are a number of different strategies that you can adopt to invest in property. Some involve owning or controlling property assets, whilst others allow income generation from working with investment properties, as we shall see.

Here is a starting list of common potential property investment strategies:

1. Single-let Buy-to-let (BTL)
2. Houses of Multiple Occupation (HMO)
3. Short-term rentals by the room or by the day/week (STR)

4. Buy-to-sell (Flip)

5. Off-plan purchase

6. Renting space at own home such as a lodger, car parking space, storage space, etc.

7. Sub-letting from the owner (Rent-to-rent)

8. Renting from the owner with option to purchase (Lease option)

9. Value-added refurbishment or 'Forced Appreciation' (VAR/FA)

10. Small scale development projects

11. Large-scale development projects

12. Lease extensions

13. Planning gain

14. Title splitting

15. Change of use (may involve planning permissions and conversion works)

16. Joint-venture partnerships (JV)

17. Pay-as-you-go type of projects to sell on or refinance later using instalment contracts, delayed completion or vendor finance

18. Deal or lead sourcing

19. Project management

20. Property letting & management

> Making money from property comes through using money, time, knowledge / experience and contacts. For example, with standard buy-to-let, the most commonly understood method of investing in property, this in the most part combines combining money and knowledge / experience…probably over a long time! However, contrast that with buy-to-sell (flipping property), where profit is made by using money, knowledge / experience over a much shorter time.

If we have no or little money to start investing, then we could consider alternative methods of making money through property, such as through sourcing deals for other investors for a fee, managing property projects or lettings on behalf of other investors, or more creative strategies such as lease options and rent-to-rent.

There are ways in which we can rely mostly on knowledge / experience and potentially contacts, such as with planning gain, title splitting, legal changes (like lease extensions) or change of use or more creative purchasing structures such as delayed completion and instalment contracts.

Finally, we can combine virtually any or all of these property-investing strategies with joint ventures. With a joint venture, we collaborate with another person(s) to provide complimentary or supplementary abilities to either plug gaps or add to overall project solution than going it alone could provide.

For some further reading on these strategies, visit the blog www.thepropertyvoice.net/blog

To help determine your preferred strategies, use the Property Strategy Selector excel spreadsheet by the same name from the **Property Strategy,** email us at admin@thepropertyvoice.net. Complete the section on the sheet and if you do not want to guess the results, simply return the completed sheet to us by e-mail to admin@thepropertyvoice.net and we will send you a summary of your ideal property strategies by return. It is not a binding commitment to follow (or not) a particular strategy but it should help frame your thoughts.

Here is a sneak peek of the strategy selector:

Property Strategy Selector	Instructions: Simply enter the number 1 in column C for each statement that applies to you	
	Return completed form to admin@ thepropertyvoice.net to get a summary of your matching strategies	
Prompts	Definition	Enter Response Here (Select all that apply)
Funds / equity available 1 to 6 months		
None	Little or no available funds	
Low	Enough for 25% deposit + fees	
Med	Enough for 50% deposit + fees	
High	Could buy a property + fees in cash	
Incremental Funds / equity available within 1-2 years		

None	Little or no available funds in future	
Low	Can save / release equity for 25% dep + fees	
Med	Can save / release equity for 50% dep + fees	
High	Can save / release equity to buy property + fees in cash	
Credit rating / financable		
Poor	Will have difficulty getting finance in own name due to credit challenges	
Average	OK rating but the odd challenge to overcome (eg self-emp, renting, etc.)	
Good	Perfect credit raing	
Knowledge / experience		
Low	Newbie, maybe read a bit, no investment properties	
Med	1-3 investment properties, some training	
High	4+ props or undertaken many projects & some training	
Time available	**Hrs pw av**	
Low	<2	
Med	2 to 8	
High	8+	
Returns sought - Income/Capital		
Income	Mainly cash today	
Capital	Mainly cash tomorrow	
Both	Combination	
Hands on / Work life balance		
None	Passive, hands-free, 'armchair investor'	
Low	Can do one or two small tasks	
Med	Willing & able to undertake a few different tasks	
High	This will be my full time job	
Returns - Time Horizon		
Short	1- to 3 years	
Med	3 to 10 years	
Long	10+ yrs	
Attitude to Risk		
Low	Set and forget, you want to sleep well at night	
Med	Can tolerate some ups and downs	
High	In for a penny, in for a pound	

Section 2
Property Investing Criteria & Calculations

In this section, we shall be addressing running the numbers and cross-checking a potential or existing deal against some Key Performance Indicators (KPIs).

Why do we need to do this? Well, if we do not know what we are aiming at then how will we know if we have a good deal or a bad deal when presented with one? Equally, if we already own property, how can we tell how it is performing in relation to our set criteria and targets, our other properties and even against potential new alternatives? Knowing what our criteria are and how to run the numbers is essential in evaluating our property investment performance.

Applying the KPIs to our own property investments

I have developed a couple of deal calculators for both standard buy-to-let and also, buy-to-sell or 'flips'. These are available to download from this KPI link, email us at admin@thepropertyvoice.net for the link. Drop me a line if you need some help or guidance in using these. The BTL one especially may be tricky, as it has the provision for refinancing after undertaking some works.

In addition, it is useful to set some criteria for evaluating a property invest- ment – these will be your KPIs. In the example spreadsheet, again available the KPI link (email us at admin@thepropertyvoice.net for the link), I have set up some criteria of my own. A score of 1 entered into the right hand column suggests a deal meets this individual criterion. The closer the total score to 100% the better the deal fits your stated criteria. Clearly, it all begins with setting YOUR own criteria…that is the most important part.

Use and adapt these checklists to fit your own investment criteria in order to quickly assess a potential property against the Key Performance Indicators that are important to you. Then use the calculators to evaluate the returns of your investment properties or deal opportunities.

For further reading on investment criteria based on my 'STAR Matrix': com- muter towns, school catchment areas, train commuting maps & employment mapping.

For further reading on understanding investment returns and how to cal- culate them: BTL investment returns, how to become a property developer, the rental yield illusion, five common financial traps, Rodney, you plonker!, costings, cashflow, ROI & cash margin & my top 3 metrics.

All of these articles can be found at www.thepropertyvoice.net and using the search feature, or just email us at admin@thepropertyvoice.net for the full links.

Appendix - Definitions of some of the most common property investment KPIs:

Gross Yield = total annual rent before deductions / current property valuation

Note: I always use the current valuation on the bottom of this calculation to give a true reflection of this measure as it relates to the current market. Some people use purchase price instead but for me that is not as accurate a comparison. The result is expressed as a percentage.

Net Yield = total annual rent less all annual operating costs / current property valuation

Note: all operating costs including mortgage interest (not capital payments), letting agent fees, insurance, regular checks (gas safety, EPC. Etc.), repairs and maintenance & void periods (non-payment of rent). The result is expressed as a percentage.

Net Annual / Monthly Cashflow = total annual rent less all annual operating costs (/12 for monthly equivalent)

Note: the net annual cashflow is the total annual rent less all of the operating costs of running the property (mortgage interest, letting fees, insurance, maintenance, voids, etc.). Total cash invested into the deal calculated by adding up ALL cash costs (not added to a mortgage) associated with purchasing the property. These could include cash deposit (or full purchase price if not using a mortgage), refurbishment and conversion works, broker, lender and solicitor fees, sourcing fees (if applicable), etc. The idea is to capture all £s invested in pure cash terms. The result will be a percentage and you can then set yourself a target to aim at with your investments, property or otherwise. The result will be expressed as a positive or negative £ value

Return on Investment = net annual cashflow / total cash invested into the property

Note: the net annual cashflow is as per the definition above. Total cash invested into the deal calculated by adding up ALL cash costs (not added to a mortgage) associated with purchasing the property. These could include

cash deposit (or full purchase price if not using a mortgage), refurbishment and conversion works, broker, lender and solicitor fees, sourcing fees (if applicable), etc. The idea is to capture all £s invested in pure cash terms.

Return on debt = net annual cashflow / outstanding mortgage balance

Note: this is a great measure to use to see how sensitive you are to interest rate movements on the mortgage debt. The result is expressed as a percentage and so this percentage will give an indication as to by how much the mortgage interest rate can go up before the property is in a negative cashflow position

Section 3
Property Investing Research Tools

When we are considering investing in property, it is ~~important~~ essential that we undertake adequate research or due diligence before we proceed. This section provides an overview, or introduction to the issue. More research / due diligence may be required beyond the content of this section therefore.

Some people approach research from one starting point and others from a different one. For example, I recently mentioned an opportunity to a business partner and he dived straight into the local area detail, whilst my starting point was the commercials (the numbers). Neither approach was the right one to begin with – as long as we end up covering all the necessary bases before we commit to anything. In the example of the property I mentioned,

my business partner and I did cover all of the bases required...and thankfully drew the same conclusion.

Personally speaking I have a range of criteria that I like to check off initially (see Section 2) and so this is where I begin myself. If I get enough ticks in the box, then I will proceed to the more in depth research and due diligence as my next steps.

With a standard buy-to-let, my starting criteria (you should set your own) are broadly as follows:

1. **Population** – in my case an urban area with more than 100,000 people living in it.

2. **'STAR Criteria'** – STAR stands for Schools (and universities), Transport links (road, bus, rail, etc.), Amenities (shops, leisure, public services, etc.) & Revenue (jobs, local economy and investment). This is broad ranging and varies according to my tenant profile, so it is hard to summarise fully here. Needless to say, I check a few thinks quickly on the first pass, such as time to the nearest form of transport relevant for my target tenant (so bus stop, main road/motorway junction or rail station say), local supermarkets, local employment levels and employers and also the schools for family lets or Uni for students.

3. **Rental Demand** - I check for strong rental demand, quickly done on one of the property portals such as Rightmove & Zoopla. What I do is a search under rental properties in my target range; so similar style, number of bedrooms and rental range as the target property. I can see how many listings there are and if I then select let agreed included I can get a feel for the local supply and demand by comparing the number of properties in each (ideally looking for higher proportions with let agreed). I then use Zoopla to see average time to let stats with the local agents, which gives me a feel for the rental demand and likely void period I could expect. More than 60 day's to let is poor.

4. **Opportunity to add value** – again tricky to list everything I check at face value but I am looking for cosmetic improvements, refurb projects, extension, conversion or development opportunities. I check photos, nearby properties for precedents (e.g. loft conversion, extension, etc.), floor plans for reconfiguration options and so on.

Problem properties (subsidence, rot, Japanese Knotweed, etc.) can also offer opportunities but best avoided if you are less experienced.

5. **Opportunity to recycle my funds** within x months – building on 4. above, this is where I assess how much each pound I spend and how much of an improvement in value this could achieve. I tend to target a £2+ return for each £1 spent on improvements. I also benchmark the end-value, after works against similar properties nearby. One guide to recycle most of my deposit and works funds quickly is to work out the end valuation x 75% to give me the refinance amount and then deduct my fees and costs to leave me with what I should be paying for the property ideally. It is just a guide and often I will leave a few pounds invested in a property.

6. **Minimum equity target** – I have my own target as to how much equity gain I would like to achieve. I achieve equity gain by a combination of buying at a discount to similar properties nearby and / or by adding value in some way as mentioned above. The portals (Rightmove & Zoopla) are a great resource here.

7. **Financial analysis** (gross yield, net yield, ROI & cashflow) – I use the calculator I shared in Section 2 to plug in the estimated numbers here. The entries come from experience, actual figures (such as mortgage quotes) and local comparables.

Assuming a property gets past these headline criteria then I would proceed to the next steps.

Some more aspects to research (again, not an exhaustive list):

1. THE LOCATION – this is the immediate vicinity of the property, the town/ city centre and the local authority area itself. Things to look for include:

   a. Crime rates, local demographics and social factors

   b. Transport connections (building on what I mentioned above, calculating commute times, etc.)

   c. Schools and universities

   d. Neighbours – state of their property, disputes, amenability to renovations / refurbishment and tenants.

e. Alternate views of the property and area – maps, street views & Google Earth views

f. Local employment factors (employers and unemployment levels)

g. The local economy and any large infrastructure projects

h. Environmental factors such as flood risk, mining area, refuse & recycling centres and such like

i. Planning & licensing restrictions

2. THE PROPERTY

a. General condition, lick of paint or complete refurbishment? State of the electrics, plumbing & heating, windows & doors, roof & guttering, etc.

b. The structure – cracks, roof, additional works, full survey required?

c. The layout – is it optimised for best value? Could we add a bedroom, relocate a downstairs bathroom, extend, change use, etc.?

d. Outside and outbuildings – gardens, garage & parking, sheds & outhouses, etc.

e. Broadband speed and other utilities

3. SUPPLIERS & BUSINESS PARTNERS – this means people involved in making the deal happen such as: agents/sourcers, builders/trades, professionals/advisors and so on. I want to know who I am dealing with and depending on the level of engagement would consider vetting and validating many of these people using the following means:

a. Referral and recommendation from people I know, or in my wider network, themselves with a good reputation. Similarly and where relevant, ask to speak to existing, recent customers for another insight.

b. Undertaking a Google search on any individual and / or company involved (in the latter case, also the fellow directors / partners). Look out for negative press and use the word 'scam' or 'review' in the search term. Go at least 3-5 pages deep as some people are very good at burying bad news!

c. Check up on duedil.com and / or Companies House as to current company trading position, any negative credit information and associated companies / directorships - look for patterns of corporate failure

d. Check on property forums for experience good and bad, noting that this is not always the most reliable source if you don't know and trust the sources

e. Meet people face-to-face and at their premises if possible to verify they are who they say they are and check the way they are organised

f. Do a mystery shopper exercise, especially with letting agents. See how they treat prospective tenants as well as landlords.

> **One final word that surpasses all is…learn to get in touch with and trust your gut instincts. Should this not be a strength of yours then I highly recommend getting close to and seeking input from someone that you do trust that has good gut instincts instead – an experienced investor, mentor or professional.**

For some further reading on these research and due diligence, visit the following: Get Rich Quick, Research Trades People, Property Club Scams, Become a Property Millionaire, Richard Brown Property Geek Interview, Property118 Research Tool, Location Research, Experience & Wisdom in Property and of course, The Property Voice Resources page.

All of these articles can be found at www.thepropertyvoice.net and using the search feature, or just email us at admin@thepropertyvoice.net for the full links.

Appendix: Property Research – Prompts, Tools & Resources

All of these articles can be found at www.thepropertyvoice.net and using the search feature, or just email us at admin@thepropertyvoice.net for the full links.

❖ **Portals**
- Zoopla
- Rightmove
- Prime Location

❖ **Other listings**
- Gumtree
- Spareroom
- home.co.uk
- White Hot Property
- Mouseprice
- RightYieldUK

❖ **Market Info**
- Estate / letting agents
- Surveyors
- Brokers & solicitors
- Infrastructure & construction projects

❖ **Prices & valuations**
- Sold / let prices
- Portals
- Land Registry
- Mouseprice
- Nethouseprices
- OurProperty

- Asking prices
- home.co.uk
- Portals
- Current values
- Zoopla
- Mouseprice
- Hometrack
- Land values
- Knight Frank Residential Development Land Index

❖ **Area stats & info**
- Crime Stats
- Check My Area
- Property Notepad
- Pure Location
- Property Wizza
- Find a Hood
- Neighbourhood Statistics
- Streetcheck
- Acorn
- RealHub
- SamKnows
- Checkmyfile

❖ **Mapping**
- Streetmap
- Google Maps
- Street View
- Google Earth

Please send additional suggestions for inclusion
to admin@thepropertyvoice.net

Section 4
Property Reading & Communities

Let us start with property communities...

It is great to hang out with fellow investors, to learn, share our experiences, find answers and get support for what can at times be a lonely journey. Therefore, I have pulled together some of the more prominent property communities out there, both face-to-face and virtual in nature... Just email us at admin@thepropertyvoice.net for the full links.

- **Property forums & communities**

  - Forums: Property Tribes, Property 118, The Property Hub

  - Social media groups & pages (e.g. Facebook, Linked In, Google+)

  - Online networks (subscription): PIN Academy, Progressive Property

  - Offline networks: PIN meetings, PPN meetings

  - Event listings (Incl. meetings mentioned above): Just Do Property, My Property Power Team, Your Property Network

- **Industry bodies**

  - Landlords: NLA, RLA

  - Lettings: ARLA

  - Ombudsmen: The Property Ombudsman, Property Redress Scheme, Ombudsman Services

  - Finance: FCA, CML, NACFB

- **News channels**

  - National press (on/offline – The Telegraph and This Is Money are particularly good)

  - Social media groups & pages (e.g. Twitter, Facebook, Linked In, Google+)

  - Industry press (sales, lettings, finance)

  - News feeds / portals: RSS, Scoop.it, Blogs

  - Newsletters: Email opt-ins at popular blogs and websites

  - Magazines: Property Investor News, Your Property Network, Buy to let magazine

  - New media: Podcasts, Youtube, Webinars

Action step: why not join a property forum, a social media group or two, subscribe to some of the news feeds / email lists and attend one or two property meetings? Immerse yourself into the property world for a few weeks and be enriched ☺

Now to property reading material...

> Reading is like food for the brain. When we read, we expand our knowledge, learn to see the world through another's eyes and can let our imagination run free. If were able to read just one book a month, then in 5 years we would have read 60 books…imagine what riches we would discover over this period…

Where to start though…how about here…my top 5:

I was recently asked to give my top 5 essential property books by Vanessa Warwick from Property Tribes…here is the blog post on Property Tribes & The Property Voice…so to my list:

"Rich Dad, Poor Dad" – taught me the value of assets and passive income

"The Richest Man in Babylon" – simply explains the keys to long-term wealth creation

"Man's Search For Meaning" – if you don't have a clear purpose then you have nothing…and be grateful for what you do have!

"The 7 Habits of Highly Effective People" – personal development and growth in yourself is perhaps the greatest investment of all

"How to Get Rich, Not Quick" – we need a plan to save money to invest and this little known and low cost book does exactly that.

After tackling that appetizer, we can move onto the starter course…

Personal development stalwarts – it all begins in the mind...

Feel the Fear and Do It Anyway – **Susan Jeffers** | How to Win Friends and Influence People – **Dale Carnegie** | The Power of Positive Thinking – **Norman Vincent Peale** | Think and Grow Rich – **Napoleon Hill** | Reinvention: How to Make the Rest of your Life the Best of Your Life – **Brian Tracy**

Life, values & meaning…what is it all for…it might change the way you see yourself and the world?

The Long Walk to Freedom – **Nelson Mandela's biography** | This Will Never Happen Again – **David Cain**

Personal finances: yes, we need to save some money for property investing (most of the time)…

30 Day Money Plan: Take Control of Your Finances in Just 5 Minutes a Day – **Damien Fahy, Paul Arnot**

Property…ah yes that's why you came here!

Property Magic – **Simon Zutshi** | The 44 Most Closely Guarded Property Secrets – **Rob Moore & Mark Homer** | Hustle Your Way To Property Success: Love It Or Hate It. . .There's No Inbetween – **Paul Ribbons** | HMO Property Success the Proven Strategy for Financial Freedom Through Multi-Let Property Investing – **Nick Fox** | Property Investment for Beginners – **Rob Dix** | Successful Property Letting: How to Make Money in Buy-to-Let – **David Lawrenson** | Beyond the Bricks – **Rob Dix** | Terrible Estate Agent Photos – **Andy Donaldson** | The Complete Guide to Property Investing Success – **Angela Bryant** | How To Buy Property at Auction: The Essential Guide to Winning Property and Buy-to-Let Bargains – **Samantha Collett** | Dominate Your Ground: Essential Skills of a Property Trader – **Mark I'Anson**

Property investor magazines…so lighter read with regular property insights…

Your Property Network | Property Investor News | Landlord & Buy-to-Let Magazine

OK, so we have worked our way through an appetizer and starter course…so, to the main course feast…are you ready for this…check out the extended reading list of seventy books in the appendix below.

…And if you have any room at all left for desert then why not pay a visit to Jayne Owen's Property Bookshop to see what else takes your fancy, or Steve Bolton from Platinum Property Partners Top 50 recommended books

Nowadays there are several ways to consume books – regular ol' paperback/hardback of course but we also have digital readers, such as the Kindle and now even audio books available through providers such as Amazon's Audible as well. As a new user of audio books, I now find myself with three different books on the go at the same time: paper, Kindle & audio version. This allows me to accelerate my reading consumption and make good use of 'downtime' to increase my knowledge.

Action step: Why not set yourself a reading goal?

During my twenties, I was reading around a book every two weeks on average over a few years and this helped to catapult my learning and development. I am more up and down these days due to my writing commitments and other forms of information consumption, however if we were to commit to a book every two weeks then we would have read every book mentioned here in forty-four months.

To help break it down into bite-sized pieces:

- GOAL #1 - The top 5 'appetiser' course in just 10 weeks

- GOAL #2 - The top 5 'appetiser' & the 'starter' course in 52 weeks / a year

- GOAL #3 - All 96 books on this list…a veritable feast…in 192 weeks, which is less than 4 years to read more books than a university student would read to get their degree…now, that is a property education!

Even if you read just one book a month, you will have covered Goals #1 & #2 in just over two years.

Appendix: Property Books – Additional Reading (Extended List)

1. Key Persons on Influence, Daniel Priestly
2. Building Wealth, Russ Whitney
3. Positive Thinking, published by Essential life skills
4. Who Moved My Cheese, Dr Spencer Johnson
5. Trump; Strategies for Real Estate, George Ross
6. The Slight Edge, Jeff Olson,
7. You and Your Money, Alvin Hall
8. The Automatic Millionaire, David Bach
9. The Secrets of the Millionaire Mind, T. Harv. Eker
10. The Millionaire Next Door Dr Thomas Stanley
11. The Millionaire Woman Next Door, Dr Thomas Stanley
12. Price the Job, Sarah Beeny (a bit old, but a basic)
13. The Greatest Salesman in the World, Og Mandino
14. Cashvertising by Drew Eric Whitman
15. 22 Immutable Laws of Marketing
16. Tested Advertising Methods by John Caple
17. Contagious: Why Things Catch on by Jonah Berger
18. Agile Results by J.D. Meier
19. The Power of Full Engagement by Jim Loehr and Tony Schwartz
20. Procrastination: Why You Do it, What to do About it Now by Jane Burka & Lenora Yuen
21. The Twelve Week Year by Brian Moran & Michael Lennington
22. Good to Great by Jim Collins
23. The One Minute Manger, Malcom Gladwell

24. Tim Ferris, 4 Hour Work Week

25. Wallace D Wattles, The science of getting rich.

26. The Ikea story, bio of Ingvar Kampard

27. Warren Buffett's biography, Roger Lowenstein

28. How to Get Rich by Felix Dennis

29. How to Fail at Almost Everything and Still Win Big by Scott Adam

30. So Good They Can't Ignore You by Cal Newport

31. Drive by Daniel Pink

32. Rework by 37Signals

33. The Toyota Way by Jeffrey Liker

34. Losing my Virginity, Richard Branson

35. Your Wish is my Command, Kevin Trudeau

36. The Compound Effect, Darren Hardy

37. The Persuasion Skills Black Book, Rintu Basu

38. The Trumps, Gwenda Blair

39. Tycoon, Geoffrey Wansell,

40. SPIN Selling Fieldbook, Neil Rackham,

41. Creating a Bug Free Mind, Andy Shaw,

42. 10 Second Philosophy, A practical Guide to Success and Happiness, Derek Mills

43. The Greatest Salesman in the World, Brian Tracey

44. How to Talk to Anyone, Leil Lowndes

45. Mastering Your Hdden Self, Serge Kahili King

46. Concentration, Theron Q. Dumont

47. Influence: The Psychologogy of Persuasion, Robert Cialdini

48. Advances Selling Strategies, Brian Tracey

49. The Magic of Thinking Big, David J. Schwartz

50. The Art of the Deal, Donald Trump

51. What to say when you are talking to yourself, Shad Helstetter

52. Live Your Dreams, Les Brown

53. Eat that Frog, Brian Tracey

54. Just Listen, Mark Goulston

55. Goals, Brian Tracey

56. Stop thinking Start living" by Richard Carlson.

57. How to Change Your Life, Benjamin Bonetti

58. Your Pension Shortfall, Your Rescue Plan, Gill Alton

59. Success Principles by Jack Canfield

60. Brick Buy Brick series from Tigrent Learning

61. Property Chain: The Definitive Guide to Buying or Selling, Renting or Letting, Building or Improving Your Home – Annie Ashworth & Meg Sanders

62. Flash Boys, Michael Lewis

63. The Great Game of Business, Jack Stack

64. The Fish that Ate a Whale, Rich Cohen

65. Mastering the Rockefeller Habits, Verne Harnish

66. Get Sh*t Done, Niall Harbison

67. Crush It by Gary Vanderchuck

68. The Millionaire Fastlane by DJ DeMarco

69. Gerald Ronson biography - Leading from the front

70. Wage Slave to Financial Freedom by Neil Mansell

Send in any additional book recommendations to admin@thepropertyvoice. net

Credits: I have collated the long list of books mentioned in the appendix above from a variety of sources, including my own. However, a large chunk of these book recommendations also came from Susannah Cole of The Good Property Company and also Rob Dix, Rob Bence & a number of willing contributors from The Property Hub…thank you very much indeed for all of your contributions.

Section 5
Lettings & Property Management

To be frank, this is such a diverse and wide-ranging area that touches on so many different aspects of our responsibilities as landlords and property investors that I could not do the subject full justice within the scope of this document.

However, what I can do is signpost you to a range of resources that you can review to ensure that you are fully compliant with the law and ideally also with 'best practice', so that we can raise rental standards within our communities, ensure we have excellent long-term property investments and keep our tenants satisfied at the same time. These are contained in the Appendix.

My personal approach to lettings & property management

I have a strong view on this subject.

A new or inexperienced landlord / investor (defined as owning 2 or less rental properties) should do one of two things before considering renting out property:

Option 1 – Use the services of a good, reputable letting agent (member of both an industry trade body and redress scheme)
And / or
Option 2 – Get accredited by one of the main landlord associations (NLA or RLA) if planning to self-manage

The reason for adopting this stance is that this is a serious business, with many laws and other responsibilities. To go in with an amateurish approach is simply asking for trouble…or at worst could result in a disaster (financial, legal, accidental or even fatal at the extreme). Do not risk being an amateur; it really is not worth it and it costs so little to protect ourselves.

I have a double-digit rental portfolio myself and choose to use the services of letting agents to manage all of my properties. I am therefore an outsourcer by choice BUT this does not absolve me from any responsibility towards my tenants and properties. If there is a problem or fault on the part of the agent, it will still be my legal responsibility, possibly theirs too but still mine all the same. Therefore, I adopt an attitude of managing my agent, to ensure they are correctly managing my property. I want to be able to sleep well at night.

Lettings & Property Management Top Tips

Here are some of the essential steps that I take when managing a property using an agent; nearly all apply equally to self-management:

1. Work with reputable agents that are ideally members of their trade body (ARLA) but definitely part of a redress scheme, which became law on 1st October 2014. Price is important but value for money and professionalism are worth far more to me. The most I pay an agent for full management in a single let is 11%, the least is 7% but I would place a far higher emphasis on using a trustworthy, knowledgeable and professional agent than a cheap one. Do read the letting agent's terms and conditions carefully to avoid being caught out by hidden fees.

2. What is the right tenant for my property? This is the right question at the wrong time - it should be asked before buying a rental property. When looking to buy, we need to know who will rent it. Singles/couples/families/sharers? Executive/White Collar/Blue Collar/Students/Benefits? Young/Old/Abled/Disabled? Long-term/short-term? Home/holiday rental/business-related? The standard of finish and rent level needs to reflect the answers to these questions.

3. Ensure that the property is presented to an acceptable and habitable standard. Tip: if let in a good condition it attracts better tenants and encourages them to look after the property. Always ensure the property is safe and legal above all. In terms of standard of finishing, this should be in line with your target tenant group and unless in high-end, fully serviced apartments not high-end finishes, as you might put in your own home.

4. Advertising of lets tips. The advert must list any fees that the tenant could be asked to pay, have good photos & descriptions to let faster and put the listing on a main property portal (ideally two). Set the rent level at 95% of the market rent on first-time lets and at tough times of year (e.g. August & December) consider doing a promotion (fee-free, first week free, etc.).

5. Always do a written inventory with phots and take meter readings.

6. Check that all utility companies and council tax notified of moving in/out dates by the agent and <u>not</u> the tenant.

7. Make sure the property has a valid EPC (10-yearly) and gas safety certificate (annual); whilst electrical checks are not mandatory (except in HMOs), I would advise a PAT test on any appliances periodically (every 3-5 years depending on age, usage, etc.). A visual inspection of electrical circuits etc. should happen each year or on change of tenancy also.

8. Have smoke detectors and ideally carbon monoxide detectors installed.

9. If letting furnished, check that all furniture complies with The Furniture & Furnishings (Fire) (Safety)(Amendment) Regs 1993.

10. Undertake full tenant assessment & referencing to clude affordability & ID & immigration status checks, previous landlord, employer,

credit search references and possibly also a 'lifestyle reference' from Landlord Referencing.

11. Have a properly drawn up Assured Shorthold Tenancy Agreement (AST), guarantors (if required) along with mandatory deposit protection through one of the three approved schemes and always ensure the Prescribed Information issued to the tenant within 30 days.

12. Insure the property with a good quality landlord insurance policy. Cover should include landlord liability, rebuilding cost and loss of rent in event of fire or destruction, legal protection fees, landlord's contents (this includes appliances, flooring, kitchens and any fixtures/furniture – this all adds up) and for me always malicious damage protection. If the property is a flat then the buildings insurance is covered under a block policy but landlord's contents insurance including all apart from the building is still advisable.

13. Consider rent guarantee insurance RGI), especially if only a small number of properties are owned. I self-protect my portfolio by setting aside 3-4 weeks rent, per property, per year to cover voids and arrears but RGI can cover extended arrears and non-payment and legal fees, which can add up to a tidy sum if necessary (note: it takes around 4-9 months to evict someone currently). However, check the policy, as like all insurance – cover, exclusions and excesses vary.

14. Ensure that the tenant knows the essentials like appliance manuals, heating and water controls, location of water stop-tap & fuse box, repairs & maintenance reporting issues, inspection frequency, utility providers, bin collection days and any other aspects relevant to that property. Equally, tell them & in writing their primary responsibilities being: paying their rent on time, looking after the property and being a good member of the community (noise, parking, etc.). Most eviction causes fall into rent arrears, property misuse/damage and anti-social behaviour.

15. Undertake regular inspections at least every six months but ideally every three months. Flex this after the first one or two based on experience for each tenant but I would not recommend less than six-monthly – make sure the first inspection is within the first three months regardless. This is to set the tone and to protect yourself against horror stories like the property becoming a cannabis facto-

ry or something like that. However, do remember that this is your tenant's home, so leave them in peace and always give notice before visiting.

16. Keep your own records of the property and tenancy including: mortgage details (Incl. any fixed term expiry date), names of tenants, date moved in and term of tenancy, rent payable, key dates (EPC, gas safety, etc.).

17. Keep good accounts / bookkeeping records of each property, detailing all income and expenditure (<u>always</u> get a receipt!). Make sure you notify HMRC that you are now renting out properties as a) you must declare this as a business in advance and b) you must complete a tax return and pay any tax due. Use a spreadsheet or specialised property management software and / or an accountant to ensure you are fully compliant here. Set up a separate bank account for rent receipts and property expenses; it will make life so much simpler.

18. Respond to and fix repairs and maintenance issues promptly and fairly. <u>Budget for these expenses</u> – they will come! Allow at least 5% of the annual gross rent or the cost of a boiler replacement, whichever is higher, as a contingency fund (could be more depending on age and condition of the property). Discuss issues that cause problems with the property on the tenant's side if necessary, such as condensation causing mould. Encourage the tenants to report issues such as leaks, blocked gutters, damage and such like…it is our investment we are talking about here.

19. Use trustworthy, reliable and recommended <u>tradespeople</u> to undertake works in the property. I adopt a three-pronged approach here when <u>working with an agent on repairs</u>. First, I tell them what expenses I will authorise without referral, usually up to £100. Then, I ask them to get a second quote on larger expenses of say £100 to £500. Finally, I ask them to get three quotes for large jobs above £500 say. I also reserve the right to take over and source my own tradespeople for large jobs.

20. If there are problems, like non-payment of rent, then good communication and a problem-solving approach works best. Cannot pay? - understand their issue and agree a payment schedule. Untidy

properties is not your problem but faulty or damaged ones are… talk and put things right early. Use a similar approach to anti-social behaviour. If all goes wrong then stay on the right side of the law at all times, document things clearly in writing, do not threaten but explain their responsibility, your expectation and any consequence to their actions. Enlist a specialist like Landlord Action if the worst happens and eviction is required.

21. If a tenant wants to leave early – let them! However, explain that they may need to cover the agent re-letting fees and will be responsible to pay the rent until the property is re-let.

22. Refresh the properties between tenancies, or periodically and plan for major refurbishments or updates as far in advance as possible. Agree any works access with the tenants in advance.

23. Work with an existing tenant should they be vacating, to ensure viewings take place before they leave – consider incentives to encourage them to collaborate, such as £50 credit if let before they leave but do not use their deposit as part of any incentive.

24. Be prompt and fair in dealing with deposit return – if the tenant responsibilities are clearly pointed out at the beginning, a good inventory is in place and a property visit is undertaken prior to departure (highlighting any issues that need putting right, like cleaning, repairs, etc.)…then there should not be much debate around return of or deduction from the deposit. Do a property check out and crosscheck against the inventory – the biggest cause of disagreement here for me is cleaning (carpets, cooker and kitchen/bathroom), so highlight the expectation before they leave. Consider returning deposits in full if only small issues remain…this just helps to improve people's perception of us!

25. Undertake rent reviews periodically but not during the term of a tenancy agreement, if longer than 1 year then you can agree annual reviews. Whilst, maximising our rent is part of our objective do consider these points: a) better a good tenant paying 90% to 95% of the market rent than a bad one not paying and; b) remember that each month a property is empty between lets costs us 8% in lost annual rent, so voids really hurt us. I usually do not increase the rent for the first two years of my tenancies, unless I had to let it cheaply

at the beginning for some reason.

26. Check the tenant's intentions well before the expiry of the tenancy, will they extend or leave? If they plan to leave then start remarketing the property at least two months in advance, we need to work with the existing tenants on this for viewing access of course but make sure this is in their tenancy agreement and talk to them through it.

I know it is not exactly a <u>short</u> list but hopefully a <u>helpful</u> one all the same ☺

Property investment can be a highly rewarding long-term investment strategy but at the same time, it is a business providing a service to paying customers (tenants). Equally, there are lots of legal and other responsibilities that we need to take care of. This should not to put us off, merely let us simply make sure we do things the right way...we are not in the rogue landlord brigade here! Email us at admin@thepropertyvoice.net for the full links.

Appendix: Lettings & Management – Additional Links & References

Let us start with the newly released Private Rented Sector Code of Practice, which is a cross-stakeholder collaboration of both mandatory (must have) and ideal (nice to have) practices for us to adhere to. Check it out to see what is expected of us.

Next, Kate Faulkner has developed something of a specialism for checklists, among other things. Pay a visit to her website for easily digestible property rental checklists on a range of different aspects of operating as a compliant landlord.

Some other useful sources of information with regard to letting and managing a property are available from the following organisations:

Shelter – not exactly 'landlord-friendly' at times but this is more balanced and shows both sides

The Government – mostly our legal responsibilities

Landlord Blog / Life – a colourful outlook from a fellow property blogger, this section is excellent and breaks down the detail very well

Some additional references from me:

Landlords beware: 5 common financial traps

Be a terrible cashflow investor

Saving money by being a DIY, self-managing landlord

Vetting a letting agent

Property damage and how to protect from it

Letting to tenants with pets

Furnished properties earn up to 35% more rent

A minor tenancy saga is unfolding

Section 6
Property Financials

I am a big supporter of running an investment property portfolio (and each individual property) as a business operation and so, I thought it fitting to use an analogy from the business world to illustrate some of these aspects more fully. The year-end accounts of a business becomes my basis of illustration therefore.

A standard set of accounts for a business will include these individual items:

1. **Balance Sheet** – showing assets and liabilities
2. **Profit & Loss Account** – setting out income & expenditure
3. **Cashflow Statement** – detailing the incoming and outgoing of funds
4. **Contingencies** – setting out things that might happen in the future
5. **Accounting Systems** –not a part of the main accounts but we need to keep a record of all the numbers to effectively manage our business.

Taking these headings in turn:

1. Balance Sheet

A balance sheet sets out <u>assets</u> and <u>liabilities</u>.

An asset is something we <u>own</u> of value. For most buy-to-let investors, the biggest asset(s) will be the property or properties themselves. Most businesses will record assets based on what is called 'lower of cost or net book value', which is accountant speak for the lowest value something is worth in reality. However, with assets like property, we get to record them based on what they are worth on the open market and this could in fact be higher or lower than we paid for the property.

Property prices are moving all of the time following the market cycles. Prices go up and down but history has shown us that over the long-term (meaning say 15-25 years), then they tend to go up.

We may have other assets in our property portfolio, such as 'white goods' and furniture if we provide these, although they will in the most part a) be a small percentage of our total asset value and b) be a depreciating asset…usually requiring replacement at some point in time.

Similarly, to the definition of an asset, a liability is something we <u>owe</u> of value. For most buy-to-let investors, the biggest liability will be a mortgage or other debt secured on the property. The correct way to record the value of a liability is to show the balance outstanding to the lender in our accounts. However, as we shall see when we discuss contingencies, there could be extra amounts payable under certain circumstances, such as early-repayment charges / penalties. For now though, let us keep this illustration simple and ignore these.

We can calculate our <u>net asset position</u> by deducting our liabilities value from our asset value. For example, if we have a property that costs us £100,000 to buy and we use a mortgage of £75,000 to help fund the purchase and ignoring everything else for now, we would have net assets of £25,000. We could also call this net asset value '<u>net equity</u>'. Had we bought the property with cash instead, then our net asset position would instead be £100,000.

One further point on assets is the notion of capital expenditure (<u>capex</u>). Capex is where we spend / invest money on an item that will enhance or

maintain the value of an asset BUT where we cannot claim it as an operating expense (opex) as far as HMRC is concerned (my definition here). This may appear complex at first, especially when we look at the differences of balance sheet, profit & loss and cashflow. Some examples of capex are:

- Buying and selling fees, such as legal, survey, stamp duty
- Structural works expenditure like an extension, loft conversion or knocking down walls
- 'White goods' (new kitchen appliances)
- Some costs relating to replacement IF there is a significant upgrade over and beyond keeping up with current standards

The difference in classification between capex and opex is an important one. For example, opex can be offset against rental profits to reduce income tax, whereas capex cannot and instead only offset against capital gains – applicable when we sell the property, which could be decades in the future…or never.

However, it is never as simple as this and this is where the importance of understanding financing principles will stand us in good stead. For example, as I mentioned, the asset values fluctuate and the mortgage settlement figures can have extra charges added to them. This means our business has uncertainty and this uncertainty can carry certain risks, as we shall see.

Equally, an asset usually requires some kind of maintenance or upkeep to preserve the best value and so there are costs of owning a property – which will be our expenditure. However, the good news is that the asset should also generate money in the form of rent for buy-to-let (BTL) properties or sales values for property trading (flipping) – these will be our revenue. We will now turn our attention to these categories.

2. Profit & Loss Account (P&L)

Also called an 'Income & Expenditure Statement'. The P&L is where we record all of the revenue (or income) that our property business generates and our expenditure (operating expenses or 'opex'), related to managing the business.

Typically, revenue will consist of rental income with a BTL or the sales proceeds of a property where we trade it instead. There could be other forms of revenue, such as cleaning and fees if applicable but these will not be significant.

Operating expenses are best summarised as all of the allowable costs attributed to generating that revenue. A list of expenses can get quite long and can include both direct and indirect expenses.

Some examples of <u>direct</u> operating expenses:

- Mortgage interest (<u>not</u> the monthly capital repayment)
- Letting agent fees and expenses
- Repairs & maintenance
- Replacement of existing contents of the property (<u>not</u> including significant structural works)
- Costs related to financing the property (including arrangement & settlement fees but <u>not</u> including buying or selling related fees)
- Voids & arrears (i.e. when we do not actually receive any rent, say when the property is unoccupied or if a tenant simply does not pay)

Some more <u>indirect</u> operating expenses are:

- Travel and mileage
- Professional fees and expenses (<u>not</u> related to the purchase or sale)
- Training (to develop an existing skill but <u>not</u> a new one)
- Print, post & stationary
- Telephone

Put simply, if we add up all of our revenue and then deduct all of our operating expenses, then we will arrive at either a <u>net profit</u> or <u>net loss</u> for each year. Some years will be better than others and in general, the biggest expenses will arise when we either buy, sell, refinance, or refurbish the property. However, as said, some of this is capex and cannot be offset against rental profits.

3. Cashflow

What exactly is cashflow? You may have heard the saying:

> **'Revenue is vanity, profit is sanity but cashflow is reality'.**

To put it a different way…just as a human needs oxygen to live, so too does a business need cash to survive. Cash is therefore like oxygen to us - as such,

it forms a major part of my investment strategy. Almost every business that goes bust (including property businesses) are due to a lack of cash ultimately.

The two major challenges we face with this concept are: a) failing to understand the difference between paper 'profits' and cashflow and; b) failing to take into consideration that with cashflow, timing is EVERYTHING.

Cashflow measures all the <u>inflows</u> and <u>outflows</u> of cash in our property business. These in/outflows could be balance sheet-related, or P&L-related. Cashflow is not concerned with how the money is allocated; it only matters whether it is money coming in or money going out…and when.

At the simplest level, here is an example of a cashflow statement when we buy and start renting a property for say the first year (let at month three):

Description	Cash In	Cash Out	BS / P&L
Buy £100k property with 75% mortgage	£75,000 (mortgage) + £25,000 (own funds)	£100,000	BS
Legal fees £1,000		£1,000	BS
Lender arrangement fee £2,000		£2,000	P&L
Light refurbishment £3,000		£3,000	P&L
New & updated kitchen £3000		£3,000	BS
Mortgage interest payment £312 / mth * 12		£3,744	P&L
Rent £550 / mth * 9	£4,950		P&L
Letting agent fee @10% of rent +VAT * 9		£594	P&L
Total	**£104,500**	**£113,338**	**(£8,838)**

As we can see from this simple illustration, our annual net cashflow was (£8,838).

However, we needed nearly all of this cash very early in the year, hence my point about timing. We would need cash funds available of £34,936 before earning a single penny in rent from this investment. Of course, this is also a simplistic example for illustration only and excludes a lot of the detail of a real situation.

4. Contingencies

The idea of looking at contingencies is to determine what might happen and attach a financial value to it…the 'what if' scenario if you like. By undertaking a 'what if' exercise, we are in effect undertaking risk analysis and by doing so we can make contingency plans according to what we believe is likely or reasonable.

Here are some of the main 'what ifs':

- House prices go up or down?
- Interest rates go up or down?
- My tenant does not pay, or damages the property?
- I cannot let the property quickly or cannot get the rent I thought?
- There is a large maintenance or repair bill?
- Financial & credit conditions improve or relax?
- I need to sell the property quickly?
- I need to settle the mortgage early, any charges to pay?
- My personal circumstances change (job loss, illness, etc.)?

Given, the response to these questions, we should then take some decisions and this should mean setting aside an additional sum of money to protect ourselves in this eventuality – I call this a 'slush fund' (or contingency fund).

We can also reduce our risk in a number of ways, such as taking out insurances, fixing our mortgage rate, upgrading a new property purchase to a decent standard, undertaking preventative maintenance (e.g. servicing), etc.

I would suggest, depending on the level of risk mitigation that we apply, that we need to set aside anything from 5% to 20% of the gross annual rent as a 'slush fund'. See this article for more context on the reasons for this.

This is of course about protecting the downside risk, of course some of these 'what ifs' could also present upside opportunities…which we can take these as they arise.

5. Accounting Systems

I will keep this part short – we absolutely <u>must</u> keep accurate financial records of all our properties and related financial activity. We need original receipts or invoices and retain these for at least six tax years for potential inspection by the tax authorities. We should consider using some form of record-keeping system, whether that is a bookkeeping journal, a spreadsheet or a bespoke piece of software that is now more available.

> I would advise using an accountant, experienced in property, ideally a property investor himself or herself. Even though there is an expense attached to this, they: a) know their way around the tax laws and; b) should be able to save money in tax by utilising all fair and legitimate means. If nothing else, they should make sure we pay what we owe in tax, on time and that just means sleeping easier.

Before I finish, I will briefly mention taxation. Despite what we might calculate as 'profit' or 'capital gain', there are some strict rules that HMRC applies in order to determine what is allowable from a tax perspective. Tax is a detailed area, which requires specialist advice from a professional advisor and is beyond the scope of this toolkit but being aware of the basics, and then doing a bit of homework could be a worthwhile activity.

The appendix goes into a little more depth in terms of understanding the differences between accounting treatment in the balance sheet, P&L and cashflow statement to give more perspective.

Regardless of the dry nature of this aspect to some, keeping a tight grip on the finances will be the foundation of a sustainable property business capable of surviving twenty to thirty years or more.

Email us at admin@thepropertyvoice.net for the full links.

Appendix: Financial Analysis (detail)

Going back to the example we shared in the **Cashflow**, section 3 above, we can take a closer look at some of the numbers.

What would be our net asset position?

In this example: £21,000 (property cost less legal fees, kitchen & mortgage balance). As far as HMRC is concerned that would be right but in reality it could be different due to what the property would actually be worth and allowing for any mortgage early repayment charges.

Our gross annual revenue position is simple: £4,950

What would be our profit / loss position?

In this example: £4,388 net loss (gross rent less, mortgage interest, letting fees, light refurbishment & lender fee).

In the simplest of terms, our investment would look like this after a year:

Balance Sheet Summary

(A) Total assets (purchase price less cost of capital works):	£96,000
(B) Total liabilities (mortgage):	(£75,000)
(A) – (B) Net asset position:	£21,000

P&L Summary

(A) Revenue:	£4,950
(B) Expenses:	£9,338
(A) – (B) Profit / (Loss)	(£4,388)

Note: this 'tax loss' can be carried forward and offset against future profits, meaning no tax to pay until the losses are covered.

Cashflow Summary

Net annual cashflow in / (out):   (£8,838)

Peak cash (outflow) balance (by month 3):   (£34,936)

There are many different figures to get our heads around, however that we must!

Section 7
Property as an Investment

Trust me, I could probably write a book on this subject…in fact I might just do that sometime! In the meantime, the intention here is merely to introduce some of the key investment principles that I consider and to cross-reference back to Section 2 of the Investor Toolkit where we looked at key performance indicators (KPIs). The key concepts I would like to outline here are:

1) Leverage & cash-on-cash return

2) Compound growth & inflation

Our KPIs in Section 2 focus on the immediate returns on our investment and as I explained, are essential to us property investors. However, if we look at the 'wealth creation', another set of investment principles come into their own. These are leverage, cash-on-cash return, compound growth and inflation.

> By wealth, I mean an accumulation of assets generating a passive income sufficient to fund our lifestyle expenses forever. If we seek true wealth as per my definition, then it is essential that we understand these concepts and learn how to apply them to our investment portfolio.

1) Leverage & cash-on-cash return

LEVERAGE – is the concept of using somebody else's money to grow the size of our investment fund. The most common example with property investing is a buy-to-let mortgage, where we add funds from a lender to our own deposit to buy a property with the combined fund value.

CASH-ON-CASH RETURN (COCR) – as per my definition of return on investment (ROI) in the KPI section of this toolkit. This is the amount of money we make on the actual cash amount of our own personal funds invested, expressed as a percentage.

Many highly wealthy people appreciate how these two concepts are related, can affect each other and then actively apply them.

A simple example may help to illustrate – let us use the same example that we used earlier in section 6.

Example property deal

Purchase price	£100,000
Deposit	£25,000
Mortgage	£75,000
Other <u>cash</u> costs to 'get into the deal' (fees & cost of works)	£9,000
Annual rent	£6,600
Annual opex (mortgage interest plus letting fees, ignore works)	£4,536
Annual opex (with no mortgage)	£792
Annual net rent (with mortgage)	£2,064
Annual net rent (without mortgage)	£5,808

LEVERAGE

Our leverage is the ratio by which we increase our cash investment in relation to the asset value. In our example here, it would be 4:1 excluding costs (£100,000 to £25,000) or 2.94:1 including all our costs (£100,000 to £34,000).

Put another way, we can multiply our investment funds from £25,000 (or £34,000) up to £100,000 by using leverage.

However, as a cautionary note, just as leverage can magnify our investment returns, it can also magnify our losses. Therefore, a safety net calculation that I use when using leverage is that of '**return on debt**'. Return on debt is the annual cash returns before interest payments as a percentage of the mortgage balance. In my example, I used a mortgage interest rate of 5% and so I would be looking for a return on debt in excess of this to make the borrowing worthwhile. My rule therefore is:

> Return on debt exceeds my mortgage interest rate by >=x%

Personally, I use 3% as my minimum value for 'x' here but you set your own comfort level.

CASH-ON-CASH-RETURN (COCR)

Our COCR is the net return on our actual cash invested. So, on a full year basis our net return here would be: £2,064 / £34,000 (I always include all expenditure in this calculation) = 6.1%

Had we not taken out a mortgage the COCR would have been: £5,808 / £109,000 = 5.3%

For now, the COCR excludes any capital growth, which I see as a bonus but in fact is where we really generate true long-term wealth (note for later).

By looking at the COCR without taking into account capital growth, we can compare our returns with many other investment alternatives (e.g. bank savings). However, if we want to accurately compare against all other asset classes (e.g. stocks and shares), then we do need to factor in capital growth into our calculations…as tricky as that can be, as illustrated when looking at buy-to-let investment returns.

What can we conclude by looking at leverage and COCR? Well, we can see how by using someone else's money we can:

a) Actually increase our asset values and;

b) In many cases, also increase our overall returns.

For example, consider the same maximum investment fund of £109,000 that we have here. We can have one investment property paid in cash or three (technically 3.2) using mortgages for the same starting investment fund. The annual investment returns would be £6,617 or £5,808, with or without a mortgage and that is before we even look at capital growth.

My rule here is to set a minimum COCR target for my investments and test each one before entering and then again every year.

2) Compound growth & inflation

COMPOUND GROWTH

'Compound growth is the eighth wonder of the world' according to Albert Einstein, who goes on to say, 'those that understand it earn it, whilst those that do not pay it'.

Compound growth - compound growth is: interest added to interest. If we had an interest rate of 3% per year and started with £10,000 we would earn £300 in the first year. However, rather than that same £300 in the second year (called 'simple interest'), we would in fact earn £309 instead. That extra £9 is the compound interest we get, or the interest on the interest. £9 might not sound like too much but if we projected that same rate of growth for-ward by the typical mortgage term of 25 years, then our £10,000 starting fund will have grown to £20,938… a 209% return on our cash compared with £17,500 or 175% if all we got was simple interest of £300 each year with no compounding. That extra 34% is the total value gained purely by compound interest. That is impressive.

INFLATION

Inflation – is a reflection of the purchasing power of money over time (i.e. in 'real terms') and is actually another form of compounding. Inflation either increases or decreases the value of our money depending on whether it is an appreciating asset or not. When faced with a choice of investment options, one rule for capital growth that I look for is:

If capital growth rate exceeds inflation, then my assets are growing in 'real terms' & if below, then my assets are shrinking in 'real terms'.

That is why if we simply hold our cash on deposit (or under the mattress), earning less than the rate of inflation then it is eroded by inflation's power. The good news is that over the long-term, the combined returns (income and capital returns) from property have exceeded 12% (of which roughly 7% is capital growth); whereas inflation has averaged 3%, which suggests that property can be an inflation beater if history repeats itself.

Another factor that inflation can influence is by reducing the real terms value of our debt in a similar way. To explain, in our example, we had a mortgage of £75,000, so applying a 3% inflation rate would effectively erode its real terms value to £35,820 in today's equivalent money. In other words, it more than halves the real terms value of our debt over time.

Wealth Creation – Putting it all together

As I stated, wealth creation to me is to build an asset-based portfolio that generates a passive income to fund our lifestyle expenses forever.

Step one – determine The Number

First, we need to establish how large our asset value needs to be – I call this 'The Number'. In the simplest of terms, The Number calculated as follows:

Total annual lifestyle expenses x 25

For example, if we have annual expenses of £20,000 then we would need a total net asset value of £500,000 to fund our lifestyle for the rest of our lives. I have written more on 'The Number' but for now, we at least have a target to aim at. Note that my calculation take no account of any pensions (state or private). I find this a safer way to set The Number but in reality, we could also reduce the lifestyle expenses figure by the amount of any fixed / guaranteed annual pension value…but remember is anything really fixed?

Next, we need to work out how to achieve a net asset value that meets The Number. If we start with a sum of money and we can estimate the average

COCR including capital growth (also assuming we re-invest all profits), then we can apply some maths to work it out.

<u>Step two – determine when this we need it</u>

This could be our normal retirement date, or an earlier or later date depending on our plans.

There is a financial rule called the Rule of 72. This rule applies the principle of compound interest to tell us how long it takes a sum of money (our net assets) to double assuming a certain rate of return.

The rule is as follows:

72 / interest rate = time to double the investment or

72 / time to double the investment = interest rate

For example, if our annual rate of return is 5%, then it would take 14.4 years for our money to double in value. However, at 10% the time taken to double the funds would be 7.2 years.

Putting it a different way, we can calculate how many years using a specific starting fund it would take to achieve The Number. For example, if we wanted to achieve this £500,000 figure above assuming a 5% interest rate, we know that our asset value would double every 14.4 years. This would mean, we would need the following starting fund based on different investment holding periods:

- £250,000 over 14.4 years
- £125,000 over 28.8 years
- £62,500 over 57.6 years

You get the picture…but many people will say one of two things:

1) I do not have £62,500 now and / or

2) I cannot wait nearly 58 years.

What then?

We have three basic options:

A) Reduce The Number and so our lifestyle

B) Save more to add to and grow our investment fund over time

C) Invest in better returning assets to accelerate the time to reach The Number

Caution: with C) I would not advocate gambling, whether that is literally gambling or investing into high-risk investment schemes. Also, please note that nothing I say is intended as financial advice, please consult a suitably qualified financial advisor for any financial advice.

The idea is merely to use some tools to see how much is needed and by when. In reality, we will not have the desired initial investment fund that will generate The Number that we would ideally like when we would like it and so we would need to add to our investment assets as time goes by. For example, we may be able to save up and buy one buy-to-let property every five years say. In that case, we could use the Rule of 72 to see when the value of each property would double using different growth rates (remembering to deduct any mortgage value from the result). It is just a guide however.

Step three – set some asset acquisition targets

With standard buy-to-let property we would usually always need to raise a deposit of c25% of the property value plus fees and other purchase related costs, so nearer 30% in reality. This will require a committed savings plan and I would definitely encourage that to happen.

However, as I outlined in Section 1 – Strategy, there are many ways to generate money through property. For example, with lease options or rent-to-rent we could reduce the starting investment significantly, or by deal sourcing, project managing or managing lets for others we can convert our time & skills into money. Similarly, if we recycle our funds by adding value, invest in higher cashflow HMO properties, or undertake development projects, then we can generate funds to set aside to invest in longer-term investment assets. And finally…

"He who has a why to live can bear almost any how." Nietzsche

Therefore, it matters less about 'how'; it matters more about 'why'…

It is important to have a clear picture of why we want to invest at all. Is it to have a pension, retire early, pay off debt, leave an inheritance, travel the world, give to family, support good causes, or just have a great time? That decision is yours but thinking it through and have a clear mental image of it will help immensely.

Once we know the 'why' (purpose) and have the 'what' (The Number), we can then set about working out the 'How' (strategy). Things will change along the way and how we start might not be how we finish but at least start we should. Having an understanding of the investment principles outlined in this section will help to guide and shape our direction and I hope will make us appreciate that acquiring income-generating assets is the key to building long-term wealth.

By understanding applying the principles of leverage, cash-on-cash returns, compound growth and inflation we will be better equipped to look at how they affect our long-term wealth creation and take action accordingly.

Email us at admin@thepropertyvoice.net for the full links.

A final thought: wealth creation rarely happens overnight (no 'get rich quick'); it usually takes years, if not decades of dedicated application of sound investment principles, repeated consistently by patient investors. I learnt this the hard way…

Summary
Investor quick start & next steps

"Knowledge is power? No. Knowledge on its own is nothing, but the application of useful knowledge, now that is powerful." Rob Liano

Over the course of this book, we have shared a series of steps from the Property Investor Toolkit. First, a reminder of what we covered, with a link to a protected section of our website with the content, the password is: **TPVToolkit:**

1. Property investing strategy & selection

2. Property investing criteria & calculations

3. Property research & due diligence

4. Property-related reading and communities

5. Lettings & property management

We covered a lot of ground here. Property investing is a simple a concept at the basic level:

Buy or control a property to rent it or sell it for profit.

However, just like an onion, there are many layers of detail and complexity. The Investor Toolkit reveals some of these layers and provides a foundation to build upon for the new investor. Equally, more experienced investors I hope, will have picked up some new insight or resource too.

Is this the end of the learning & development? Well, of course not but the real question should be: how next to learn and grow? By signing up for the Investor Toolkit, there was some desire to develop your knowledge…more so if you actually read it and clicked on all those links within the book ☺

I started my property-investing journey back in the mid-nineties and frankly, I had no clue what I was doing back then. I understood the concept in broad terms but when faced with a couple of minor setbacks, I made the biggest single mistake of my property investment career to date – I sold up. That was because I did not fully understand the principles of Section 7 of the Toolkit, the long-term principles of wealth creation. That decision has so far cost me nearly £200,000 in lost capital growth, let alone the potential rental profits, which by now might have been a further £85,000 as a conservative number. That was a heavy price to pay for a lesson in wealth creation!

Since the mid-noughties, I became a student of property investing once again. I researched and read widely, I sought out mentors and yes, I actually invested too! Now, I have achieved my original goal of plugging the hole in my pension and I do not have to 'work' again if I do not want to; sufficient is the passive income from the portfolio to fund my lifestyle. I do not say this to boast but merely to show the way forward perhaps, to be a signpost for your future journey in property.

Email us at admin@thepropertyvoice.net for the full links.

Next Steps

When asked, what I would advise a new investor to do, I usually respond with a plan similar to this:

1. Do not invest in anything yet! Get a basic understanding of property first.

2. Undertake a 3-6 month programme of active learning & research:

   a. Read books on the subject of property investing

   b. Join one or more (but not all) of the property communities

   c. Subscribe to Your Property Network magazine

   d. Find out your local property network meetings, attend 1-2 per month and chat to the investors more than those selling something

3. Consider some formal training to build on the foundations you have learnt – no need to sign up for a five-figure intensive programme though!

4. Consider getting yourself one or more mentor(s) – I say potentially more than one, as different mentors can bring different insights. A mentor can come in various forms – even books, wise forum posters or other investors but do take care, as sometimes: *free advice will cost you nothing <u>unless</u> you act on it!*

5. Consider joining a 'mastermind' group of like-minded people operating in a common interest area, with a guided facilitator ideally.

6. Decide what you want from property investing, your 'why' or purpose, then quantify this, your 'what' ('The Number') or goals and then, your ideal 'how' or strategy to achieve these

7. Finally, take action and make a start, you will learn as you go and if you also have a trusted guide or support group, you will no doubt progress faster with fewer errors along the way

How can we at The Property Voice help?

- We have insights, resources and real-life case studies on our website for you to use freely

- Review the Investor Toolkit once again to get a deeper understanding

- Drop us a line if you have a quick question: admin@thepropertyvoice.net and if we can answer it we will, or we might be able to redirect you if we cannot

We also offer various forms of learning & development through our mentoring packages:

- We have a virtual-learning programme

- An 'over-the-shoulder' observation programme to shadow experienced investors

- Ongoing coaching & mentoring programmes

- Communities & mastermind groups

Check our Mentoring page for more details of these programmes.

I urge that you do not stop the learning journey. Equally, knowledge without action and application does not create real value beyond personal satisfaction. If we learn & apply, then we grow and if we grow, the better placed we are to add more value to our lives, to those we care about and perhaps more.

Take a bit of time to reflect, dream a little if you like…imagine your life 5, 10 or even 20 years from now. Is it the life you wish for, or could it do with a bit of fine-tuning? Property investing is one way in which we can bring about a change to our future lives. All we need to do is make a start and then keep taking small steps forward. If we keep moving forward, then one day we will look back and see that we have travelled a great distance and have come a long way from where we started.

Thank you very much for making it this far; if you did, then you already show that you are more than capable of moving forward. A large number of people will sign up for this kind of resource and will at best flick through (I get the stats to back up what I say!). If you are reading this, then you are eager to learn, to grow and to apply yourself…you have a great chance of success in property investing, whether alone or with some support. Let me know if we can support you along YOUR journey!

> "Every day do something that will inch you closer to a better tomorrow." Doug Firebaugh

Richard W J Brown
Founder - The Property Voice
www.thepropertyvoice.net

Section 9
eBook only bonuses

I want to give more value than perhaps was expected, as a personal thank you for deciding to purchase this eBook version of The Property Investor Toolkit. Therefore, here are some extra 'freebies' just for you:

a) **'The Number'** – I have developed my own spreadsheet to help me determine my ideal level of 'passive income' required to fund my lifestyle and goals. It helps me to track my assets & liabilities – my personal net worth and my income & expenditure plans – my passive income target. I am happy to share this with you.

b) **Strategy Selector (results version)** – In section 1, I referred you to a link where you can download our strategy selector tool. This was the input version, which only gives half of the story – we provide the other half - a summary of your results if you send it to us. However, if you prefer to keep it to yourself, then I am happy to share the full version with you, so you can evaluate the results and preferences alone, without our intervention. I am happy to let you have the full version to use freely for yourself.

c) **Book discount** – I am in the process of completing my next book…a larger piece of work than this near 13,000-word eBook. As a thank you to purchasers of this eBook, I would be happy to offer a discount voucher to you.

d) **PDF Version of the Toolkit** - as mentioned in the Introduction, the paperback contains links best viewed in a PDF file format. The PDF version of the book includes the external links, which will come along with the bonuses mentioned above.

So, how do you get access to these eBook-only owner bonuses? Easy, just drop us a note at admin@thepropertyvoice.net along with the following information and we will send you the bonuses by return:

Your first & last name

The bonus code mentioned in the Introduction section above

Printed in Great Britain
by Amazon